Just How To Wake
The Solar Plexus

Just How To Wake The Solar Plexus
by Elizabeth Towne

ISBN 979-8-8809-0653-6

Table of Contents:

Chapter I:
I Am The Sun Of God

Do you desire above all things to live a serene, useful, successful life? Do you want to get out of the petty limitations of conventionality? Out of pain and sin and sickness? Away from the small hurts of every-day living? Do you really want to get away from them? Are you willing to work out the salvation that is in you?

Or would you rather sit still and grumble at the universe in general and everybody in particular? Do you desire health and prosperity, happiness and a wider usefulness enough to work every day and all day for them, as a man works who desires to be a great musician, or artist, or scholar? Or do you just weakly wish that somebody would carry you bodily "on flower beds of ease" to a heaven of happiness and prosperity? Are you *resolved* to have health, happiness and material prosperity, and to be more widely useful, no matter what it costs nor how long it takes?

Then you will have them. You will, without the shadow of a doubt, get there. You could not fail if you tried. And I *am* with you all the way and at the same time I *am* already there, and I will tell you something that was an immense help to me in getting there. It was the sun. Shelton says the sun is God. I should not be surprised if he is right. But I am not sure he is.

However, the sun helped me to a realization of my Self, my all-wise, all-loving, all-powerful, serenely happy Self. Your self is just as grand as my self, and you are dead certain to find your self, when once you set about it.

The reason you have not already found it is that you have put in most of your time in watching the self of other people. You have been impolite to your Self. You have consulted every Tom, Dick and Harry before your Self. And you have called your Self all sorts of names. No wonder he has crawled into his shell and pulled the hole in after him! No wonder you think he doesn't know much!

But he does, and he will do anything for you if you just be even half way civil to him! Be polite and respectful to your Self. Tell him he is a pretty good fellow after all – the best friend you have. Ask his advice, and use it. And let him do things for you. All he wants is *recognition*, and he will do anything you want done, and do it better than anybody else can do it for you.

The sun helped me to make a close acquaintance with my Self. He will also help you. Did you ever think how much alike are Son and Sun? Jesus was the Son of God. I studied the life of that Son for years, trying to be like Him. My success was indifferent.

But one day it suddenly flashed across my mind that *I am the Sun* of God! That was to me a glorious idea that took possession of me and literally transformed me by the renewing of my mind.

That is a little trick ideas have — give them a lodging and they will make a whole new house for you, a "house not made with hands."

"*I am the Sun* of God" made me all over in no time.

I will tell you some of the changes it made in me: I used to be very "sensitive"; so much so that I didn't know my own mind more than half the time; and I was always getting my feelings hurt; though I was generally too proud to show it.

I tried desperately to conquer my feelings and keep from being hurt, but success did not crown my efforts nor even perch upon my banner.

At last I grew tired of coddling my feelings and I told them, with considerable righteous indignation, to keep on feeling hurt till they got tired and quit — they would receive no more attention from me! They did get tired and quit. The sun warmed up my feelings and happified them for good and all.

This is the way of it: I said to myself, "If *I am the Sun* of Good, then my one reason for being is simply to radiate — to shine — to send out good thought."

Now, you see, that is just where I had been making a vital mistake. I had always tried to be a Moon instead of a Sun. The Moon is cold, dark, sterile, receptive, only shedding reflected light. I had been all the time receiving everything – other people's ideas and opinions, and even all kinds of hurts from them! And, as if this was not enough receiving, I daily besought God to give, give, *give* me the Holy Ghost, not to mention the hundred and one other favors I begged! – of Him and other folks.

And all this time I was really a *Sun*, the Sun of God, made for the one purpose of sending out, instead of receiving. I had "life in myself," as "the Father hath life in Himself."

In order to outgrow entirely all that sensitiveness I had simply to remember, when my feelings were injured, that I *am* a Sun made to shine, instead of a Moon made to receive hurts from without.

Every human being is literally a Sun of Good, made to radiate. If he will attend strictly to the business of sending out Good Will, as the sun radiates beams, he will soon find his feelings under his control.

Suppose every time somebody on this planet grumbled at Old Sol, he were to curl up within himself and fail to send forth his rays. If he were "sensitive" like most people that is what he would do. But Sol is too wise a god for that. He attends strictly to his own business of shining. So positively does he shine, and so fully is he absorbed in doing his best, that he shines upon not only the "just," who appreciate his shine, but he shines joyously on the "unjust," who only grumble in return. So positive is that blesses old Sol that he never feels a grumble! His shine just meets the grumble and transmutes it before it touches him.

The reason we get hurt by the unkind words of those about us is that we forget to shine.

The Sun Within

There is a real sun center in us, the Solar (or Sun) Plexus. This is a great nerve center situated in back of the stomach. When this central Sun, from which all the nerves of the body radiate, is in its normal condition, it steadily radiates a real energy, just as the sun does. This energy vibrates through the nerve highways and by-ways of the body out toward the surface of the body in all directions (the mucous membranous surface, as well as the outer skin), and is thrown off in a real halo or atmosphere, which always envelops the body. If this radiation from the Solar Plexus is positive enough, the influence of another person cannot disturb its steady, harmonious vibrations in the least.

And a person who is thus positively radiant wields an immense power for good to those less positive than himself. His presence alone, without a spoken word or even a definitely directed thought, stills the troubled minds with which he comes in contact.

In all human beings, who have not yet learned the law of being, the Solar Plexus is in a cramped condition that prevents the steady flow of life, or "nerve ether," to all parts of the body. From this

cause comes every disease of the human race —
mental, physical or environmental.

All one's "feelings" are due to the action or
inaction of this Sun-center. Good feelings are due to
free action; ill feelings to contraction. Pleasant
sensations are caused by the outflow of "nerve
ether," energy, Life; unpleasant sensations by an
interruption of the steady outflow.

In every human being there is a steady radiation
of Life, or Love, or Good Will from the Solar Plexus,
except when the individual himself interrupts the
radiation when he contracts the Solar Plexus, thus
diminishing the outflow, or interrupting it
altogether as in death.

A continued contraction of the nerves results in a
chronic state of nervous collapse. The nerves
literally collapse, as does a soft tube from which
fluid is withdrawn.

The nerves are tubes for the conveyance of Life to
all parts of the body. Contract the Solar Plexus and
you withdraw Life from the body.

The Solar Plexus is the point where life is born —
where the Uncreate becomes Create; the
unorganized becomes organized; the unconscious
becomes conscious; the invisible appears; that which
is dimensionless becomes measurable.

There is positively no limit to the amount of life
this solar center in the individual is able to
generate, and no limit to the rapidity with which it
may be generated.

But this omnipotent sun-center is a generator of blind energy, all-mighty but unintelligent in any high sense.

The Solar Plexus is a *servant* to the brain. No more life is generated (i.e., made visible) than the brain of "God in the highest" dictates. Every minute contraction and expansion of the sun-center of Life is in obedience to the brain. No lightest fancy of the brain but is responded to instantaneously by the Solar Plexus.

Do you perceive why and how it is that "of every idle word shall ye give account?" And how ye shall be "rewarded according to the deeds done in the flesh?"

What you sow in imagination you will surely reap in the body. What you have sown in thought you are reaping now.

Conscious thought is master of the sun-center, from which flows the life of your body; and the quality of your body, including the brain, determines the quality of your environment. You are your own lord and master, the arbiter of your own destiny.

Now do you see why a "sensitive" person gets "hurt" continually? He thinks he is a Moon instead of a Sun; he receives from others words or tones or acts which displease him; he contracts the sun-center of himself, stopping his radiation of Good Will.

"It is the stoppage of his own radiations of life or good will that hurts him, *not* the thing that was said or done. And he alone is the Lord of that

Sun-radiator; therefore he hurts himself. I made this discovery by actual experience, and have demonstrated the fact that nobody on earth has the power to "hurt my feelings." By studying the action of the real sun and remembering that I *am the Sun of God*, I quickly learned the art and acquired the habit of shining. "What I do ye may do also."

Chapter II:
The Lord Our God Is A Consuming Fire

Did you ever notice that the sun makes no special effort to destroy that which is not fit to live? The same steady shine which gives life to the growing plant causes fermentation, death and transmutation to everything which is cut off from the source of its life.

As soon as I learned that I am the Sun of God I knew that I need make no special effort to destroy "evil" – the "carnal mind." I saw that I had simply to shine, like Old Sol, and the radiation from me would transmute mind and body and environment for me.

That conception afforded me infinite relief. I saw that all the good I had been so assiduously endeavoring to force into myself was already mine if I would only "let my light shine" to ripen it.

I discovered also that to let my light shine is a matter of choice, not feeling, so I chose to let the light shine out from my solar center and I abandoned myself to that radiation. No more worry for me over "evil" thoughts or acts. I just let the Sun shine upon them.

I discovered that Jesus of Nazareth had a level head – "I say unto you that ye resist not evil," is the very acme of wisdom.

I had pondered often and long upon that injunction of His, without being able to see the philosophy of it, and I simply could not obey it.

Why? Because *I am good* and must, from the compulsion of my own law of being, be forever "set over against" evil. If I know no better way of getting rid of evil than to fight it, then fight I must. But the more I fight the greater the evil will grow.

At last in sheer despair, I may be still and think; when I shall see that non-resistance will conquer where resistance worse than fails.

Do you see yet why this is so? The Solar Plexus is the radiating center of life, the center from which flows the divine energy, love, that can overcome (cause to "come over") all evil. We can overcome evil with good; we can love our enemies into friends; we can "overcome' them; i.e., cause them to "come over."

Please remember that love is not sentimental gush; it is not a matter of words; but it is a steady radiation of good will from the solar center, and may or may not be expressed in word or deed. But it will be expressed in either word or deed as the need of the "enemy" calls it forth. But whether expressed or not, that steady, silent radiation of Good Will, or Love, will transmute enemies into friends, "evil" into good, just as certainly as the sun rays will make pure that which was impure.

This being true, the one thing necessary is to let the solar center radiate Good Will all the time.

Until we understand and take control of ourselves, every thought that passes through the mind affects the action of the Solar Plexus. Thoughts that are pleasant to us cause the center to open and radiate Good Will or Love. Every unpleasant thought causes it to contract, thus shutting off the supply of good will, love, life, from the body, brain and environment.

Non-resistant thought expands the Solar Plexus; resistant thought contracts it. Now do you see what a good scientist Jesus was?

"And I say unto you that ye resist not evil." If a man would have you go a mile with him, go two miles willingly; let your Good Will radiate; and by the time you have finished your second mile his Solar Plexus will be vibrating with yours, and you will both be the wiser and more loving for your journey.

But that will depend upon how you take his invitation or command. You can go under protest, asserting your own righteousness and his injustice; in which event he will conquer you, and you will have obeyed the letter, but not the spirit of Jesus' injunction.

Or you may envelop yourself with the air of a martyr – which is mighty thin covering, by the way – and go with him because it's your "duty" to do a lot of unpleasant things you would much rather leave undone. This is the air lots of women assume with their husbands and children – the injured air. They go a mile – oh, yes, two miles, or three – with their brows uplifted and their lips pursed up with "prunes and prisms," and a very loud humility of manner. All of which brings the inconsiderate husband or children to time – for a time. They feel that they have committed the unpardonable sin, and hasten to humble themselves and make amends. But by and by they become hardened – and the last state is worse than the first. You see it is not so much the thing you do as the way you do it.

I said, before we understand and take command of ourselves, every thought passing through the mind either expands or contracts the solar center of being. We must learn to control the action of the Solar Plexus just as we learn to control the action of the fingers in learning to play the piano; by thought and careful exercise.

Anybody can play the piano who will, and anybody can learn self-control who really wants to. And when he really wants to he will. Until that time you might just as well let him alone. As long as a man prefers to let his Solar Plexus flop around like a weathercock on a squally day, registering all the silly, thoughtless or malicious things his neighbor may say, why just let him flop. He will get tired of such buffetings by and by, and begin to control himself and his "feelings." Nobody can do it for him.

"Practice makes perfect." He who puts in the most time in faith-full practice will accomplish most in the shortest time. The man who puts in an hour a day in practicing "concentration" exercises and then lives the remainder of his time on the old plane of resentment and resistance, will not make half the progress of the man who spends little or no time in "exercises," but endeavors to put his good will into each act and thought of the day, every day in the week.

Every experience, little or big, is an "exercise" for developing concentration. You no more need special hours for the development than a cat needs two tails. Put your mind and good will into what you are doing, and re-put it every time you catch it flying the track.

Make up your mind to keep your light shining, your solar center expanded, no matter what happens or how you feel." Of course you can't do it at first, any more than you can play the piano by simply "making up your mind" to do it. Your hands will get out of position and your fingers will persist in being thumbs; but, nevertheless, if your mind is made up, you will keep at it until you teach your hands to keep their correct positions and your fingers to touch the keys daintily and truly, with scarcely a conscious thought.

Just so with the Solar Plexus; by practice you can teach your solar center to radiate Good Will, no matter what is happening outside of you or within, or how much your thought may be occupied with other things.

That is heaven, where I am. And the door is wide open – with "welcome" written above.

Let your light so shine that men may see your good works: — your love-sun-shines – and glorify your *I am God* which is heaven.

Chapter III:
Just Why And Just How

The Solar Plexus, or sun center, is to the human body precisely what the visible sun is to the solar system. It is the source of all life and light; it is the manufacturer of life and light.

The sun manufactures light and heat by inhaling that which transcends light and heat. The sun breathes. It inhales "spirit" and exhales light and heat – intelligent will.

The Solar Plexus inhales light and heat and exhales magnetism; another form of intelligent will; a finer form; a more intelligent will, and therefore more powerful as well as finer.

If the sun were to cease breathing, there would be nothing left for the Solar Plexus to breathe. Life would cease to manifest. If the sun were to breathe spasmodically, only half filling itself with "spirit," then would there be a poverty of light and heat. The effect of such a poverty of light and heat you can see in plants or persons kept in dungeons.

We are wont to believe that man breathes with his lungs alone, when the truth is that he breathes with every cell of his body. And each pore of his body, inside and out, is an avenue for the transmission of sunlight and heat to the great laboratory of the body, the Solar Plexus. The Solar Plexus is the body's breathing center, where sunlight and heat are transmuted to magnetism.

All disorders of the human body and brain are due to shutting off the sun's rays before they can reach the Solar Plexus. The deep and regular breather *cannot* be sick or mentally weak.

Just one thing prevents the breath from reaching the solar center; a closing of the pores, outward and inward. A stooping position will cramp and close many of the lung pores; tight clothing will shut up not only lung pores, but others as well. But first and last and always, and with more power than is contained in all other things combined, will *the Mind* contract the pores and rob body and brain of life and light.

Fear is the great robber. Watch the effect of a single fear upon yourself — see how you cringe, shrivel and contract; see how you clinch your hands and curl up your toes; see how you expel the air from your lungs and hold it expelled; and you can guess, at least, how fear keeps you out of your own. This cringing and curling and shrinking is habit with the human race. Human beings are trained to fear past, present and future; themselves and their "enemies," not to mention their friends; trained to fear what is without and what is within; fear the devil and God, too. Is it any wonder fear is a habit, and a good, full breath an unheard of thing to the majority of human beings? The one problem of the human race is to get rid of the fears so assiduously cultivated for so many ages. No need to tell the fearless one to "breathe freely." He does it without thought of effort. As a consequence, his body is large and strong.

Every effort of the individual is for the one purpose of freeing him to breathe; to inhale intelligent will; retain it until it has rejuvenated every cell and become tinctured with the essence of his being; and to *exhale* it as still more intelligent will for the accomplishment of his purposes. Man breathes in intelligent will; focuses it within; and radiates it in new and more powerful form.

He who breathes correctly appropriates intelligence and will from the sun. The freer his breathing the greater the degree of intelligent will. He who breathes freely acts freely. He who breathes deeply thinks deeply.

Only fear prevents free thought. Only restricted thought prevents free breathing.

Get rid of fear and you will need no teaching to breathe freely.

Thought and action are one. Every thought is action, but we are not yet trained to see the finer motions of thought; therefore we say, "thought sometimes prompts action"; not realizing that *all thought is motion, and all motion is thought*

One class of thinkers says breathing exercises are a necessity to a well-balanced mind and body. Another class says only thinking is necessary – the breathing will follow. Both are right, because *breathing is thinking and thinking is breathing.*

A man can no more breathe without thinking than he can think without breathing. The instant circulation of breath ceases, that instant there is no motion. No motion is annihilation.

A thinking exercise is a breathing exercise; a breathing exercise, or any other kind of an exercise, is a thinking exercise.

An exercise well done is one in which is put *all* the thought that it can contain; an exercise half done is one unwillingly, unintelligently done. The former is correct thinking; the latter is slovenly half thinking.

Somewhere away down in the animal kingdom we used to know how to breathe. That was before we learned to be scared at God and the devil – not to mention ourselves and other people. But by scare-thinking we developed the habit of half breathing. Half breathing is a habit of the human race. That is, on the male side. The female side lives on quarter breathing; because it has been taught to fear more things than men, and because women are more apt anyway at learning. Women have learned to shrink and lean. Not content with this, they have bound their feet and hands and laced themselves into strait jackets – the most infernal machine imaginable for squeezing the Solar Plexus out of all semblance to a radiating center, and shutting off the breath of life.

All this habit must be overcome in the only way possible – by the establishment of new habits; new habits of breathing, of thinking. Remember, breathing and thinking are *one*.

Therefore I say unto you, men and women, but especially women, *breathe*. And keep on breathing until you establish the habit of full, free breathing. You people who have been trying to think yourself into the free kingdom and who wonder why you seem to make so little progress, just set to work and breathe for dear life. That will help you as nothing else will. Just the very kind of thought we call "breathing" is the thought which frees from fear. The weak, sick, timid ones are the breathless ones. Asthmatics, consumptives and nervous folks need breath and plenty of it, to heal them. And they are the very ones who will not breathe if they can get out of it. They immure themselves in hot, airless rooms and gasp and gurgle and bewail fate; because they have been for years – for generations, perhaps – trying to get along without breath. This is their habit of thought.

Well, there is salvation – a new habit of thought. Practice breathing even half as diligently as you have practiced not breathing and you work out the salvation that is within you.

I will tell you just how to begin and just how to keep at it; and if you will practice faithfully for one short month you will be thoroughly convinced. And if you will keep at it until you have made full breathing a habit of thought you will be a new creature; sorrow and melancholy, fears and fighting will have ceased forever. Energy, ambition, power, joy will have grown up in their place; your shrunken and bent body will have straightened up; you will stand with a curve extra in the small of your back, instead of with one curve at the shoulders, such as you had when you were a monkey; you will walk with a spring, on the ball of the foot, instead of coming down on your heels or shuffling along any old way; your eyes will be bright and steady and ready to look kindly into every other pair of eyes; your mouth will be straight instead of drooping at the corners as in the old wailing days, and your lips will be soft and sweet to kiss; your skin will be fresh and clear and your voice will ring out, like bells over quiet waters, instead of being smothered in your throat and tinctured with whines or snarls as of old; in short, you will be a new being, born again of the "spirit" and ready to live and love and do.

Exercises

First and foremost, be sure you have plenty of open windows in your sleeping room; no a crack at top and bottom, but wide open windows. Use a screen to prevent draughts, if necessary.

When you wake in the morning throw everything wide open; lie flat on your back with outstretched arms and no pillow and light covering or, what is better, none at all. Relax from head to foot; close your mouth; take quietly a deep slow breath, filling the lungs evenly as possible all the way down; hold the breath as long as you can without straining; then see how very slowly and smoothly you can let the breath out. Pay very particular attention to this. See how slowly and steadily you can exhale the breath. Now, "get your breath" if you need to — as you certainly will if you are unaccustomed to deep breathing — and then do it over again. Repeat this five to seven times. Take about four seconds to inhale, eight seconds for holding, and as many as possible for exhaling. Possibly you cannot hold the breath so long at first; remember not to strain. Smooth, easy, steady — these are the first essentials. Practice will lengthen the breath. At first I could not inhale longer than two seconds, hold three and exhale three or four; and my heart beat as if I had exerted myself tremendously. It was three months before I could take five successive breaths such as I have described to you.

Right here I want to tell you what a help those three months of practice were to me in vocalizing. I was always troubled with short breath while singing. Four years of voice culture did little to help me. The three months in which I first practiced this breathing exercise it so happened that I was without a piano and never sang a note. Then one was brought into the house and I sang again. In spite of three or four months without a note of practice, I sang as I had never sung before. Never was singing such pleasure. It seemed to me I could sing any phrase, or two or three, with breath to spare and with a freedom I had never experienced before in my life. Since that time I have never known the old difficulty. I am convinced that systematic breathing exercises without vocalizing are of untold value to the singer.

If you are a man, or a woman who is sensible enough or slender enough to wear no corset, repeat this exercise two or three times each day, always in the same position and with the clothing loosened. And after retiring at night repeat again. Then command yourself to sleep quietly, breathe fully and wake refreshed at the usual hour.

If you will, in spite of all the medicos and Delsartes in the land, wear corsets, why, take the breathing exercises anyway. But take them standing, in the open air, if possible, or in an open window. Get a new, straight-front corset; let it out a notch or two more than you did the old one; after you put it on pull it a-way down in front and stand so your bustle is behind, where it belongs. Then throw your shoulders back, hold your head up, look like a sweet and gracious queen, turn your eyes toward heaven and all good, and breathe. Inhale love, power, shine, life – slowly, quietly; let it thrill you and permeate your every atom of being and fill your Solar Plexus with joy; let it transmute you and be transmuted; then lower your eyes, spread out your hands wide in blessing and breathe forth quietly, smoothly, slowly, all joys to all mankind.

If you are a man, never mind about the straight-front corset – just stand like an athlete, chest out and abdomen in, and take long, strong swigs from the sun; let them exhilarate all your being, souls and body; then breathe out blessings on the world. Take two or three breaths at each exercise; exercise several times a day, in standing position if you prefer; and recline night and morning for more breathing.

If you have a special pursuit in which you desire success, remember it when you are taking these exercises. While you are inhaling a breath you are negative, receptive; while you are holding the breath you are poised ready; while you are exhaling you are positive, radiant. You are giving out life to your dominion – to all who are less highly developed than yourself, to your environment in general, to your business, to whatsoever you are interested in. Then as you exhale a breath, spread forth your hands and breathe life into whatever you desire. You can grow friends, beautiful surroundings, money, loving thoughts, wisdom – anything *you will*, by this practice. I don't care two cents whether you have faith in it or not – just do it and you will find out that what I affirm is true.

The Solar Plexus is the seat of emotion. By proper exercise of the whole breathing apparatus you may gain such control of the Solar Plexus that anger, resentment, resistance, blues, discouragement and fear will be as foreign to you as are the awkward motions you used to make when you were first learning to walk or eat. All these unpleasant emotions are due to cramping the Solar Plexus. The exercises I have just given you will free the Plexus and make you "feel good." Continued practice will establish the habit of "feeling good" – that is, the habit of feeling free.

Until you succeed in establishing a habit of feeling good you will have, as you have had heretofore, periods of depression. These will gradually grow less deep and be more readily dissipated. When you feel yourself growing depressed, for no matter what cause, break up the tendency as quickly as possible. Here is the way to do it:

Undress if possible; if not, loosen your clothing; lie down flat upon your back with arms outspread and without pillow; let go of everything mentally; inhale slowly through the nostrils a full breath; hold steady a second or two; then force the breath suddenly into the upper part of the lungs; hold there a second or two and then suddenly throw all the breath down as far as possible, at the same time exclaiming mentally to the Solar Plexus, "Wake up! Wake up!" Hold the breath down a second or two; then gradually let if flow back until the lungs are evenly filled again, hold an instant, and then see how very slowly and smoothly you can exhale the breath. Do this not over three times at one exercise and only when you are depressed. Then rise and move as if you were going somewhere and meant to get there. Get interested in what you have to do. The next time you think about your depression you will wonder what makes you feel so comfortable and full of quiet go. I have used this practice, which is my own discovery, for years; for all sorts of depressions from every imaginable cause; and never once has it failed to change my feelings entirely. It is guaranteed to cure anybody who will practice it with a will.

These directions sound complicated, but after a trial or two and a re-reading or two they will nearly do themselves, so easy and delightful will you find them and their effects. Never mind if your heart thumps a bit when you first attempt any breathing exercise. It would thump just the same after any new and vigorous exercise. Just be quiet and persist. Very shortly your hear will enter into the general enjoyment and keep as quiet as a summer morn, no matter how vigorously you force the breath up and down. This exercise properly persisted in will benefit or cure functional heart disease, as well as diseases of lungs and throat. In fact, there is hardly and ailment of the human frame which cannot be cured in this way, if the practice is kept up daily or oftener for a long enough period. Remember that the shine from your sun center is to your body what the shine from Old Sol is to plant life and planets; and these exercises establish in your solar center the habit of shining.

Chapter IV:
Breathing Technique

There are breathers and breathers and breaths and breaths, and if you happen to be one kind of a breather you might take a good many thousand breaths without doing yourself very much good. All because you force one poor little bit of a muscle to do the work of a great man large muscles.

Perhaps some of you don't know that you have in your throat the neatest little trapdoor ever was seen. You might not know it is there, and you may never have heard its name, but I'll warrant you have experienced several unpleasant sensations in your day from having left this little trapdoor open at the wrong instant. And you have probably missed a great many enjoyable sensations by closing it up at unseasonable moments.

This neat little trapdoor, that works so smoothly you hardly knew you had it, is intended for just one purpose in ordinary life – the purpose of keeping anything more dense than ozone from getting into the air passage to the lungs.

But the epiglottis is a very intelligent and obedient little servant, and I have known singers to teach it to flap up and down very fast, and so help in producing staccato tones.

Then I have known other folks to impose shamefully upon this dainty little member of the human family, which is built for light, rapid motion and not for long strains.

Strange to say, it is the New Thought people, the disciples of love, who oftenest abuse it. But they don't mean to, of course.

These new thinkers have got hold somehow of the notion that there is great virtue in holding the breath a long time. So they pump themselves full of air and batten down that poor little trapdoor and keep it down until they get red in the face, and their hearts thump tempestuously and then go pit-a-pat.

Have you gone shopping recently in some big department store and had your ears assailed by a dreadful nasal wailing the while your eyes rested upon the legend, "Don't laugh – the pigs are dying?" And then you spied the pigs blown full of air and caterwauling themselves away. Whilst the pig is full and plugged up, the membrane of which it is made is stretched to the utmost. Now take him up between your two hands and squeeze him harder and harder. If there happens to be a weak spot he will burst. Or the plug may fly out. At any rate, you will stretch his skin, and it will take more air to make him plump again.

Now, that is just the way the wrong kind of holding the breath acts on your lungs. You stretch all the tissues of the lungs and batten down the epiglottis. Then the natural, untrained tendency of the chest and abdominal muscles being to straightway expel the air, all these muscles contract about your lungs, just as your fingers contracted about the skin pig, and the entire lung tissue and air passage, as well as the little trapdoor, are strained severely. And this straining interferes with the circulation of the blood, reacting upon the heart, and, if there does happen to be a weak spot in the lungs, you invite a hemorrhage. To cap all this, you make the lung tissue flabby and lazy.

The lungs should never, in ordinary breathing exercises, be forced to hold air — not for one instant.

The lungs are a pair of bellows, which fill as the muscular walls are expanded.

It is not the forcing of air inward that expands the chest walls.

Expanding the chest and abdominal muscles draws in the air, making no more of a pressure inside the body than there is on the outside. This allows a free circulation of both air and blood, and permits perfect oxygenation.

It is not the lungs that need training to breathe. They always receive all the air that the muscles will give them room for.

And they remain expanded and free just as long as the muscles will permit.

Correct breathing is correct muscling.

Breathing practices should be muscle practices, with the trapdoor wide open from start to finish.

When you practice breathing never mind the breath. Just see how far, and evenly, you can expand your chest and abdominal muscles straight outward; how long you can hold them steadily there without pressure against the epiglottis, and how very slowly, evenly and softly you can contract those muscles again. Put your *will* into your muscles, where it belongs – put your attention into them – and you will get the knack of correct breathing.

Breathe always through the nostrils.

Don't try too hard. If you have to puff and blow after a long breath you made the divisions of that breath (inhaling, holding and exhaling) too long, and you shut the trapdoor. Try again. Breathe easily.

Breathe with a *purpose*. Did you know that the difference between a man and an idiot is the difference between a purpose and no purpose? The manliest man (woman included) is the one who has the deepest, highest, steadiest *purpose*.

The idiot breathes in short, irregular puffs, never once entirely filling or emptying his lungs! And his short, erratic little puffs go to build the thousand and one short, erratic little notions which make up his expressed self.

Aimless breathing practices are, like any other aimless efforts, beastly. Will your breath-generated power in a chosen direction. Aim with it. And see you aim high and steadily.

You can do anything you steadily purpose to do. Only vacillation can defeat you; — unless you should happen ignorantly to aim at something which would enslave the free will of another. For instance, I had a man write me once to "utterly subdue to him his wife, and make her obedient to him in all things!" Now, his wife used to be that kind of a goose, but she had positively outgrown it and left His Mightiness. And this man might breathe and speak the Word, and hire healers till crack o'doom, and that is all the good it would do him. You see he didn't aim high enough. If he had aimed to be sweet enough to win a woman's devotion, he could do it, though it might take a few more incarnations in his case. But he could get there in time. Or if he had aimed to be a successful artist, or writer, or business man, he could do it without fail, if he kept steadily at it. But he wanted to boss other folks, and other folks had sense enough to boss themselves.... I returned that man's money, and told him I gloried his wife's spunk.

Breathe rhythmically.

It is said a single dog trotting across a bridge will do more toward shaking it down than whole droves of draught horses and heavy loads. There is no rhythm to the motion of the dog.

It is said a man with a violin could shake down Brooklyn bridge by keeping up a steady vibration of the note the bridge is keyed to.

A rhythmical heart beat makes a powerful body.

Rhythmical breathing communicates rhythm to the heart and brain and gives the entire man a good time. Breathing regularly and deeply brings the whole body and brain and soul and spirit into harmony of action.

Harmony is health. Harmony is power.

Did you ever see four men, or women, take three or four long, even breaths in unison, and at the last inhalation raise with the tips of their fingers, a heavy man clear above their heads? Without those long, even breaths, that feat cannot be done.

Rhythmical breathing generates power in the body. During sleep the breathing is even and deep, and the body recuperates.

Recuperates from what? From the irregularity of action caused by the waking, the surface brain. The breathing apparatus responds to every conscious thought. It gasps with astonishment, stands still with fear, or puffs with excitement.

In the long, quiet night it recovers its natural rhythmic action.

Our breathing apparatus is like a child's untrained fingers – full of infinite capacity for the expression of beauty, harmony, power. But, like the child's fingers, our breathing apparatus needs training to work steadily, intelligently, even if the brain does get flighty or lazy. Just as each one of the child's individual fingers has to lean how to do its own work without responding to the impulsion sent to its mates, so the breathing apparatus must be taught to keep coolly, evenly at work no matter what is going on above in the brain or outside the body.

This can be accomplished by persistent practice.

Rhythmical action of the breathing machinery will keep the body full of power and prepare "a heart for any fate."

One who teaches his body to keep coolly, sweetly, harmoniously at work no matter what turns up, will cease to gasp and gurgle, faint and collapse at the very times he most needs power.

When you are "tired" or "discouraged" your body is starved by short, irregular breath supply.

Lie down flat, with arms out from the body and eyes closed. Inhale slowly, but not too slowly; just easily; as you inhale, say mentally, with eyes raised under your closed lids, "I *am*" – say it slowly and distinctly, and try quietly to realize that the Infinite is really you – "I and the Father are One." Keep the chest walls expanded for a moment and the throat open. Then slowly and very smoothly exhale the breath, lowering your eyes as you do so, under closed lids always, saying softly, lingeringly, mentally, with downward inflection, "Love." "I –*am* – Love."

Breathe rhythmically, as slowly as you can breathe easily, and always fully. Keep this up until your mind is quiet and you have forgotten all about being "discouraged" or "blue." Keep this up until I *am* consciousness has gone with the breath into the lungs, and so into the blood, and with it into all the body.

It takes about two minutes for the blood to make the circuit of the body. But in order to change your "feelings" it must make the circuit several times, setting up a new rhythmic vibration of *I – am – love*

– consciousness. Your whole being must "catch" the vibrations of that grand, peaceful, powerful I *am* consciousness. Lungs, heart, solar center and brain must pulse together with the Infinite.

This is the best "concentration" exercise I know of – the only sure means I know of for becoming conscious of the power flowing outward from the "world I *am*: into the "world I do." It is the only *infallible* remedy I know for discouragement, unrest, lack of interest, impatience, anger, malice, revenge, resentment, and the hanging on habit. And I believe it to be literally infallible for any human being who really wants to be cured of any of these negatives.

Repeat the dose every time you feel negative. At first it may take ten minutes or more to free you, but after a time, five minutes will do it. If you nip every little spell in the bud, you will soon cease to feel distinctively negative at all.

In-breath the Infinite I *am*; let it renew you, mind and body; out-breathe Love, Wealth, all you desire. Remember, you do not take in things you desire – they press out through you. You in-breathe I am, Love, God.

Never mind what the trouble is – just chop it squarely off with the practice. Keep at it. There is simply no end to the good you will get out of it. You will practice it until you get your consciousness right with the real pulses of your being – the I *am* vibrations. In proportion as you live in that consciousness, you realize health, happiness, and *success*.

Whatever breathing practices you use or don't use, remember to straighten up and take a few, full, slow breaths, whenever you think of it – no matter where you are or what you are doing. There is *life* in it and Joy.

Faith By Katherine Quinn

I sent Desire across the sea.
('Twas years and years ago)
I gave the lad what gold I had,
And vowed through weal or woe

That I'd be true unto my love
Until his journey's end,
And that each day he was away
A message I would send.
My friends all smiled to see my faith.

Then sighed, "Alack, alack,
Your only gains will be your pains,
For he will ne'er come back."
I paid no heed unto their words,
But worked on steadfastly.

When worst I fared, most loud declared
That I had ships at sea.
Last night my vessel touched on shore;
And Peace sat in her bow.
And Joy was there, and Love most fair.

And Plenty strode her prow.
Desire had brought them all to me
Across the briny foam.
"Ah, well-a-day," my friends now say,
"Who'd think that he'd come home?"

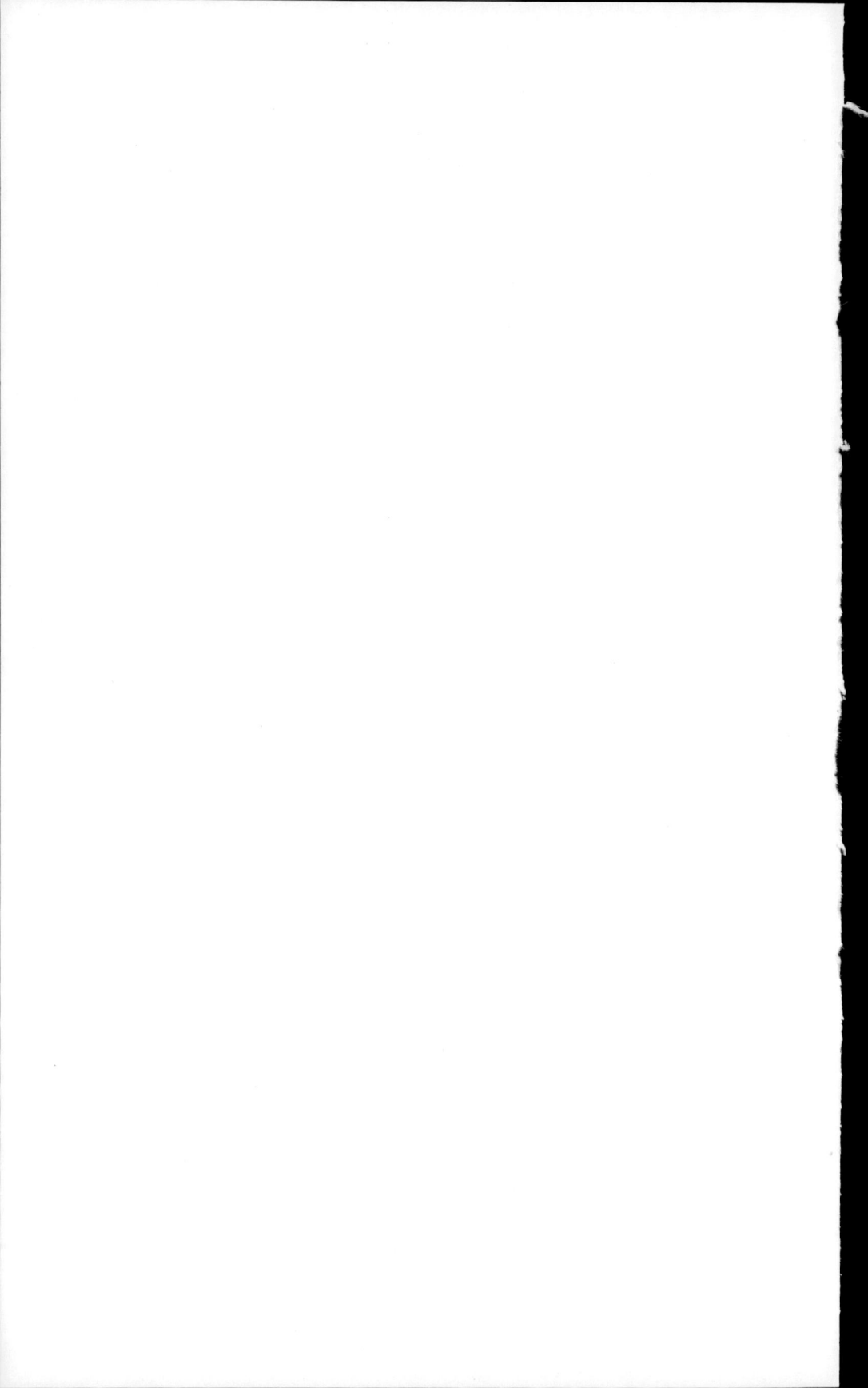